Contents

Summer Celebrations 2

No-Bake Desserts.......... 18

Fruit Frenzy 32

Frosty Treats 44

Healthy Living 56

Index 64

Summer Celebrations

Fourth of July Party Trifle

PREP: 20 min. plus refrigerating • MAKES: 18 servings, ⅔ cup each.

WHAT YOU NEED

- **1½ cups boiling water**
- **2 pkg. (4-serving size each) JELL-O Berry Blue Flavor Gelatin**
- **1½ cups cold water**
- **1 pkg. (10.75 oz.) frozen prepared pound cake, thawed, cubed**
- **1 tub (8 oz.) COOL WHIP Whipped Topping, thawed**
- **2 cups halved strawberries**

MAKE IT

STIR boiling water into dry gelatin mixes in large bowl at least 2 min. until completely dissolved. Stir in cold water. Pour into 13×9-inch pan. Refrigerate 3 hours or until firm.

CUT gelatin into ½-inch cubes. Place in 3½-qt. serving bowl. Cover with cake cubes, half of the whipped topping and the strawberries. Top with remaining whipped topping.

REFRIGERATE at least 1 hour before serving. Store leftovers in refrigerator.

Variation: Prepare as directed, using **COOL WHIP LITE** Whipped Topping and fat-free pound cake.

Patriotic Gelatin in a Cloud

PREP: 20 min. plus refrigerating • MAKES: 8 servings.

WHAT YOU NEED

- **2 cups boiling water, divided**
- **1 pkg. (4-serving size) JELL-O Strawberry Flavor Gelatin**
- **1 pkg. (4-serving size) JELL-O Berry Blue Flavor Gelatin**
- **1 cup cold water, divided**
- **2 cups thawed COOL WHIP Whipped Topping**

MAKE IT

STIR 1 cup of the boiling water into each flavor dry gelatin mix in separate medium bowls at least 2 min. until completely dissolved. Stir ½ cup of the cold water into gelatin in each bowl. Pour each flavor gelatin into separate 8-inch square pan. Refrigerate 4 hours or until firm.

DIP pans in warm water 15 sec. Cut gelatin into cubes, using sharp knife dipped in hot water. Loosen cubes from pan with spatula; refrigerate until ready to serve.

SPOON ¼ cup whipped topping into each of 8 dessert dishes just before serving. Using back of spoon, spread whipped topping onto bottom and up sides of each dish. Fill evenly with equal measures of the red and blue gelatin cubes. Store leftover desserts in refrigerator.

Jazz It Up: Top each dessert with 1 Tbsp. additional thawed **COOL WHIP** Whipped Topping just before serving.

Rocket Pops

PREP: 30 min. plus freezing • MAKES: 16 servings, 1 pop each.

WHAT YOU NEED

1 pkg. (4-serving size) JELL-O Cherry Flavor Gelatin

1 cup sugar, divided

2 cups boiling water, divided

Ice cubes

2 cups cold water, divided

1 pkg. (4-serving size) JELL-O Berry Blue Flavor Gelatin

1 tub (8 oz.) COOL WHIP Whipped Topping, thawed

MAKE IT

COMBINE dry cherry gelatin mix and ½ cup of the sugar in medium bowl. Add 1 cup of the boiling water; stir at least 2 min. until gelatin is completely dissolved. Add enough ice cubes to 1 cup of the cold water to measure 2 cups. Add to gelatin; stir until ice is completely melted. Pour evenly into
16 (5-oz.) plastic or paper cups, adding about ¼ cup of the gelatin to each cup. Freeze 1 hour.

MEANWHILE, combine dry blue gelatin mix and remaining ½ cup sugar in medium bowl. Add remaining 1 cup boiling water; stir at least 2 min. until gelatin is completely dissolved. Add enough ice cubes to remaining 1 cup cold water to measure 2 cups. Add to gelatin; stir until ice is completely melted. Refrigerate 1 hour.

SPOON about 3 Tbsp. of the whipped topping over red gelatin in each cup; top evenly with blue gelatin, adding about ¼ cup of the gelatin to each cup. Freeze 1 hour or until almost firm. Insert wooden pop stick or plastic spoon into center of each cup for handle. Freeze an additional 4 hours or overnight. To remove pops from cups, place bottoms of cups under warm running water for 15 sec. Press firmly on bottoms of cups to release pops. (Do not twist or pull pop sticks.) Store leftover pops in freezer.

Note: Wooden pop sticks can be found at craft stores.

Firecracker Bites

PREP: 40 min. plus freezing • MAKES: 14 servings, 3 wafer sandwiches each.

WHAT YOU NEED

- **1 pkg. (8 oz.) PHILADELPHIA Cream Cheese, softened**
- **1 cup cold milk**
- **1 pkg. (3.4 oz.) JELL-O Vanilla Flavor Instant Pudding**
- **1½ cups thawed COOL WHIP Whipped Topping, divided**
- **1 pkg. (12 oz.) vanilla wafers**
- **½ cup mixed red, white and blue sprinkles**
- **42 pieces red string licorice (1 inch)**

MAKE IT

BEAT cream cheese in large bowl with mixer until creamy. Gradually beat in milk. Add dry pudding mix; beat 2 min. Whisk in 1 cup whipped topping.

SPOON about 1½ Tbsp. pudding mixture onto each of half the wafers; cover with remaining wafers to make sandwiches. Freeze 2 hours or until filling is firm.

SPREAD tops of wafer sandwiches with remaining whipped topping. Dip in sprinkles. Insert licorice piece into top of each for the fuse. Freeze until ready to serve.

How to Fill Sandwiches: Spoon pudding mixture into resealable plastic bag; seal bag. Cut off small corner from bottom of bag; use to pipe pudding onto wafers. Cover with remaining wafers and continue as directed.

Note: If you have any pudding mixture left over or choose to not make all 42 wafer sandwiches, layer remaining pudding mixture in parfait glasses with fresh fruit, such as strawberries and blueberries. Top each parfait with a dollop of the remaining **COOL WHIP**.

Patriotic Poke Cake

PREP: 30 min. plus refrigerating • MAKES: 16 servings, 1 slice each.

WHAT YOU NEED

2 baked round white cake layers (9 inch), cooled

2 cups boiling water, divided

1 pkg. (4-serving size) JELL-O Strawberry Flavor Gelatin, or any other red flavor

1 pkg. (4-serving size) JELL-O Berry Blue Flavor Gelatin

1 tub (8 oz.) COOL WHIP Whipped Topping, thawed, divided

MAKE IT

PLACE cake layers, top-sides up, in 2 clean (9-inch) round cake pans. Pierce cakes with large fork at ½-inch intervals.

STIR 1 cup of the boiling water into each flavor dry gelatin mix in separate small bowls 2 min. until completely dissolved. Carefully pour red gelatin over 1 cake layer and blue gelatin over remaining cake layer. Refrigerate 3 hours.

DIP 1 cake pan in warm water 10 sec.; unmold onto serving plate. Spread with about 1 cup whipped topping. Unmold second cake layer; carefully place on first cake layer. Frost top and side of cake with remaining whipped topping. Refrigerate 1 hour or until ready to serve. Cut into 16 slices to serve. Store leftover cake in refrigerator.

Substitute: Prepare as directed, using **COOL WHIP LITE** Whipped Topping.

Patriotic Poke Cake with Cream Cheese Frosting: Pour gelatin over cake layers and refrigerate as directed. Unmold 1 of the layers onto serving plate; set aside. Beat 2 pkg. (8 oz. each) softened **PHILADELPHIA** Cream Cheese and 2 cups powdered sugar in large bowl with electric mixer on medium speed or wire whisk until well blended. Gently stir in whipped topping until well blended. Spread onto cake layer on plate as directed; top with second cake layer. Continue as directed.

Special Extra: Serve with colorful fresh berries, such as blueberries, strawberries and raspberries.

Wave Your Flag Cheesecake

PREP: 20 min. plus refrigerating • MAKES: 20 servings, 1 piece each.

WHAT YOU NEED

- **1** qt. strawberries, divided
- **1½** cups boiling water
- **1** pkg. (8-serving size) or 2 pkg. (4-serving size each) JELL-O Gelatin, any red flavor
- Ice cubes
- **1** cup cold water
- **1** pkg. (10.75 oz.) prepared pound cake, cut into 10 slices
- **1⅓** cups blueberries, divided
- **2** pkg. (8 oz. each) PHILADELPHIA Cream Cheese, softened
- **¼** cup sugar
- **1** tub (8 oz.) COOL WHIP Whipped Topping, thawed

MAKE IT

SLICE 1 cup of the strawberries. Halve remaining strawberries; set aside. Stir boiling water into dry gelatin mix in large bowl 2 min. or until completely dissolved. Add enough ice to cold water to measure 2 cups. Add to gelatin; stir until ice is melted. Refrigerate 5 min. or until slightly thickened (consistency of unbeaten egg whites).

MEANWHILE, cover bottom of 13×9-inch dish with cake. Stir sliced strawberries and 1 cup blueberries into gelatin. Spoon over cake. Refrigerate 4 hours or until set.

BEAT cream cheese and sugar in large bowl with wire whisk until well blended; gently stir in whipped topping. Spread over gelatin. Top with strawberry halves and remaining blueberries to resemble flag. Store in refrigerator.

Make Ahead: Make dessert the day before. Top with fruit just before serving.

Banana Split Pie

PREP: 15 min. plus refrigerating • MAKES: 8 servings, 1 slice each.

WHAT YOU NEED

- **2 cups cold milk**
- **2 pkg. (4-serving size each) JELL-O Vanilla Flavor Instant Pudding**
- **1 graham cracker pie crust (6 oz.)**
- **1 cup sliced strawberries, divided**
- **1 banana, sliced**
- **1 tub (8 oz.) COOL WHIP Whipped Topping, thawed, divided**
- **2 Tbsp. chocolate syrup**

MAKE IT

POUR milk into large bowl. Add dry pudding mixes. Beat with wire whisk 2 min. Spread 1½ cups of the pudding onto bottom of crust.

TOP with half of the strawberries; cover with bananas. Add half of the whipped topping to remaining pudding; stir gently until well blended. Spread over fruit layer in crust. Spread remaining whipped topping over pie to within 1 inch of crust. Drizzle with chocolate syrup; top with remaining strawberries.

REFRIGERATE 3 hours or until set. Store leftovers in refrigerator.

Healthy Living: Save 100 calories and 5 grams of fat per serving by preparing with fat-free milk, **JELL-O** Vanilla Flavor Fat Free Sugar Free Instant Pudding, a ready-to-use reduced-fat graham cracker crumb crust and **COOL WHIP LITE** Whipped Topping.

Special Extra: Garnish with ¼ cup PLANTERS Pecan Pieces just before serving.

Luscious "Cream Puffs"

PREP: 15 min. plus refrigerating • MAKES: 9 servings.

WHAT YOU NEED

- **1 sheet frozen puff pastry (½ of 17.3-oz. pkg.), thawed**
- **1 pkg. (3.4 oz.) JELL-O Vanilla Flavor Instant Pudding**
- **1 cup cold milk**
- **½ cup thawed COOL WHIP Whipped Topping**
- **1 square BAKER'S Semi-Sweet Chocolate, melted**

MAKE IT

HEAT oven to 400°F.

UNFOLD pastry on lightly floured surface; roll to 10-inch square. Cut into 9 circles with 3-inch cookie cutter. Place, 2 inches apart, on baking sheet. Bake 10 min. Remove to wire racks; cool completely.

MEANWHILE, beat dry pudding mix and milk with whisk 2 min. Stir in whipped topping. Refrigerate 15 min.

CUT pastry circles horizontally in half; fill with pudding mixture. Drizzle with chocolate.

Variation: Prepare as directed, using fat-free milk, **JELL-O** Vanilla Flavor Fat Free Sugar Free Instant Pudding and **COOL WHIP LITE** Whipped Topping.

Substitute: Prepare using **JELL-O** Chocolate Instant Pudding.

No-Bake Desserts

Strawberry-Mango No-Bake Cheesecake

PREP: 20 min. plus refrigerating • MAKES: 8 servings, 1 slice each.

WHAT YOU NEED

- **2 pkg. (8 oz. each) PHILADELPHIA Cream Cheese, softened**
- **½ cup sugar**
- **1 tub (8 oz.) COOL WHIP Whipped Topping, divided**
- **2 cups strawberries, sliced**
- **1 cup finely chopped mango**
- **1 graham cracker pie crust (6 oz.)**

MAKE IT

BEAT cream cheese and sugar in large bowl with electric mixer until well blended. Blend in half of the whipped topping. Fold in fruit.

SPOON into crust. Top with remaining whipped topping.

REFRIGERATE 3 hours or until firm. Store leftovers in refrigerator.

Jazz It Up: Sprinkle with ¼ cup toasted **BAKER'S ANGEL FLAKE** Coconut just before serving.

Summer Berry Cheesecake Pie

PREP: 25 min. plus refrigerating • MAKES: 8 servings, 1 slice each.

WHAT YOU NEED

- **1 pkg. (8 oz.) PHILADELPHIA Cream Cheese, softened**
- **2 Tbsp. sugar**
- **2 cups thawed COOL WHIP Whipped Topping, divided**
- **1 graham cracker pie crust (6 oz.)**
- **¾ cup boiling water**
- **1 pkg. (4-serving size) JELL-O Strawberry Flavor Gelatin**
- **½ cup ice cubes**
- **½ cup blueberries**
- **1½ cups strawberries, halved**

MAKE IT

BEAT cream cheese and sugar in large bowl with wire whisk until well blended. Gently stir in 1 cup whipped topping; spread onto bottom of crust.

STIR boiling water into dry gelatin mix in medium bowl at least 2 min. until completely dissolved. Add ice cubes; stir until ice is completely melted. Let stand 5 min. or until gelatin is consistency of unbeaten egg whites. Meanwhile, arrange blueberries and strawberries over cream cheese layer in crust. Cover with gelatin.

REFRIGERATE 3 hours or until gelatin layer is firm. Top each slice with 2 Tbsp. of remaining whipped topping just before serving. Store leftovers in refrigerator.

Substitute: Prepare as directed, using any red flavor of **JELL-O** Gelatin.

Variation: Prepare as directed, using **PHILADELPHIA** Neufchâtel Cheese, **COOL WHIP LITE** Whipped Topping and **JELL-O** Strawberry Flavor Sugar Free Gelatin.

Melon Bubbles

PREP: 15 min. plus refrigerating • MAKES: 8 servings.

WHAT YOU NEED

- **1½ cups boiling water**
- **2 pkg. (4-serving size each) JELL-O Melon Fusion Flavor Gelatin**
- **2½ cups cold club soda**
- **⅓ cup each: cantaloupe, honeydew and watermelon balls**

MAKE IT

STIR boiling water into dry gelatin mixes in large bowl at least 2 min. until completely dissolved. Stir in club soda. Refrigerate 1½ hours or until thickened (spoon drawn through leaves definite impression).

MEASURE 1 cup thickened gelatin into medium bowl; set aside. Stir melon balls into remaining gelatin. Spoon into 8 dessert glasses.

BEAT reserved gelatin with electric mixer on high speed until fluffy and about doubled in volume. Spoon over gelatin in glasses. Refrigerate 3 hours or until firm. Store leftovers in refrigerator.

Substitute: Substitute seltzer for the club soda.

Substitute: Prepare as directed, using 1 pkg. (8-serving size) or 2 pkg. (4-serving size each) **JELL-O** Lemon Flavor Sugar Free Gelatin.

COOL WHIP Cookie Sandwiches

PREP: 15 min. plus refrigerating • MAKES: 16 servings.

WHAT YOU NEED

- **32 chocolate chip cookies**
- **4 oz. (½ of 8-oz. pkg.) PHILADELPHIA Cream Cheese, softened**
- **¼ cup sugar**
- **1 cup thawed COOL WHIP Whipped Topping**
- **1 tub (7 oz.) BAKER'S Dark Semi-Sweet Dipping Chocolate**
- **⅓ cup multi-colored sprinkles**

MAKE IT

PLACE 16 cookies, top-sides down, in single layer on waxed paper-covered baking sheet.

MIX cream cheese and sugar in medium bowl until well blended. Stir in whipped topping; spread onto cookies on baking sheet. Cover each with second cookie to make sandwich. Press together gently to secure.

MELT dipping chocolate as directed on package. Dip sandwiches in chocolate, turning to evenly coat all sides; shake gently to remove excess chocolate. Return to baking sheet; top with sprinkles. Refrigerate 1 hour or until chocolate coating is set. Store leftovers in refrigerator.

Take Along: Pack cookies in airtight container between layers of waxed paper. Store in refrigerator until ready to pack in cooler and tote to the picnic or party.

Triple-Layer Lemon Meringue Pie

PREP: 15 min. plus refrigerating • MAKES: 8 servings, 1 slice each.

WHAT YOU NEED

- **2 cups cold milk**
- **2 pkg. (4-serving size each) JELL-O Lemon Flavor Instant Pudding**
- **1 Tbsp. lemon juice**
- **1 graham cracker pie crust (6 oz.)**
- **1 tub (8 oz.) COOL WHIP Whipped Topping, thawed, divided**
- **2½ cups JET-PUFFED Miniature Marshmallows, divided**
- **2 Tbsp. cold milk**

MAKE IT

POUR 2 cups milk into large bowl. Add dry pudding mixes and juice. Beat with wire whisk 2 min. or until well blended. (Mixture will be thick.)

SPREAD 1½ cups of the pudding onto bottom of crust; set aside. Add half of the whipped topping to remaining pudding; stir gently until well blended. Spread over pudding layer in crust. Place 2 cups of the marshmallows in large microwaveable bowl. Add 2 Tbsp. milk; stir. Microwave on HIGH 1½ min. or until marshmallows are completely melted, stirring after 1 min. Stir until well blended. Refrigerate 15 min. or until cooled. Gently stir in remaining whipped topping; spread over pudding mixture.

REFRIGERATE 3 hours or until set. Top with the remaining ½ cup marshmallows just before serving. Store leftover pie in refrigerator.

Jazz It Up: Garnish with lemon twists or ½ cup sliced strawberries just before serving.

Tropical Pina Colada Pie

PREP: 20 min. plus refrigerating • MAKES: 8 servings, 1 slice each.

WHAT YOU NEED

- **2/3 cup boiling water**
- **1 pkg. (4-serving size) JELL-O Island Pineapple Flavor Gelatin**
- **4 oz. (1/2 of 8-oz. pkg.) PHILADELPHIA Cream Cheese, softened**
- **1 can (8 oz.) crushed pineapple in juice, undrained**
- **2 Tbsp. coconut-flavored rum or cold water**
- **2 cups thawed COOL WHIP Whipped Topping, divided**
- **1/4 cup BAKER'S ANGEL FLAKE Coconut, toasted, divided**
- **1/4 cup PLANTERS Sliced Almonds, toasted, divided**
- **1 graham cracker pie crust (6 oz.)**

MAKE IT

STIR boiling water into dry gelatin mix in small bowl 2 min. or until dissolved. Beat cream cheese in large bowl of electric mixer until creamy. Gradually add gelatin, mixing well after each addition. Stir in pineapple, rum and 1 cup whipped topping.

SPRINKLE 2 Tbsp. each of the coconut and almonds onto bottom of crust; cover with whipped topping mixture. Refrigerate 3 hours or until set.

TOP with dollops of remaining whipped topping, coconut and almonds just before serving. Store leftovers in refrigerator.

Substitute: If substituting water for the rum, add 1/2 tsp. rum extract with the cold water.

Banana Cream Pie with Caramel Drizzle

PREP: 15 min. plus refrigerating • MAKES: 10 servings.

WHAT YOU NEED

1½ bananas, divided

1 graham cracker pie crust (6 oz.)

2 cups cold milk

2 pkg. (4-serving size each) JELL-O Vanilla Flavor Instant Pudding

2 cups thawed COOL WHIP Whipped Topping, divided

¼ cup caramel ice cream topping

MAKE IT

SLICE 1 of the bananas; spread onto bottom of crust.

POUR milk into large bowl. Add dry pudding mixes. Beat with wire whisk 2 min. or until well blended. Gently stir in 1 cup whipped topping; spoon into crust.

REFRIGERATE 4 hours or until set. Drizzle with caramel topping just before serving. Top with remaining whipped topping and remaining ½ banana, sliced. Store leftovers in refrigerator.

Variation: Prepare as directed, using **JELL-O** Banana Cream Flavor Instant Pudding.

Substitute: Prepare as directed, using **COOL WHIP LITE** Whipped Topping.

Fruit Frenzy

Cool Raspberry Fruit Dip

PREP: 5 min. • MAKES: 1¼ cups or 10 servings, 2 Tbsp. each.

WHAT YOU NEED

- **1 container (6 oz.) raspberry nonfat yogurt**
- **¾ cup thawed COOL WHIP Sugar Free Whipped Topping**

MAKE IT

MIX ingredients until well blended.

SERVE immediately as a dip for cut-up fresh fruit. Or, cover and refrigerate until ready to serve.

Substitute: Prepare as directed, using **COOL WHIP LITE** Whipped Topping.

Nutrition Bonus: Add extra flavor to your favorite fruit with this tasty low-fat dip.

Floating Fruit Parfaits

PREP: 15 min. plus refrigerating • MAKES: 6 servings.

WHAT YOU NEED

- **½ cup sliced strawberries**
- **¾ cup boiling water**
- **1 pkg. (0.3 oz.) JELL-O Strawberry Flavor Sugar Free Gelatin**
- **½ cup cold water**
- **¾ cup ice cubes**
- **1 cup plus 6 Tbsp. thawed COOL WHIP LITE Whipped Topping, divided**

MAKE IT

SPOON berries into 6 parfait or dessert glasses. Add boiling water to dry gelatin mix in medium bowl; stir 2 min. until completely dissolved. Add cold water and ice cubes; stir until ice is melted. Pour ¾ cup gelatin over berries. Refrigerate 20 min. or until gelatin is set but not firm.

ADD 1 cup whipped topping to remaining gelatin; whisk until well blended. Spoon over gelatin in glasses.

REFRIGERATE 1 hour or until firm. Serve topped with the remaining whipped topping.

Variation: Prepare as directed, using **JELL-O** Orange Flavor Sugar Free Gelatin and substituting cantaloupe balls for the strawberries.

Storing Fresh Fruit: Most fruits keep best when stored in the refrigerator. Berries, cherries and plums should not be washed before refrigeration, since excess moisture will cause these fruits to spoil more quickly.

Nutrition Bonus: Satisfy your sweet tooth with this elegant low-fat dessert. As a bonus, the strawberries provide a good source of vitamin C.

Special Extra: Add ½ cup seedless grapes with the strawberries.

Chocolate-Dipped Strawberries

PREP: 10 min. • MAKES: 3 doz. or 18 servings, 2 strawberries each.

WHAT YOU NEED

1 pkg. (7 oz.) BAKER'S Milk Chocolate Dipping Chocolate

36 medium strawberries

MAKE IT

MELT chocolate as directed on package.

DIP strawberries into chocolate; let excess chocolate drip off.

PLACE on waxed paper-covered baking sheet or tray. Let stand at room temperature or store in refrigerator for 30 min. or until chocolate is firm.

Variation: Prepare as directed, using **BAKER'S** Dark Semi-Sweet Dipping Chocolate. Or, substitute 7 oz. melted **BAKER'S GERMAN'S** Sweet Chocolate for the dipping chocolate.

Cooking Know-How: For best results, serve strawberries the same day they are dipped.

Substitute: Prepare as directed, using 18 large strawberries. Makes 18 servings, 1 strawberry each.

How to Select and Store Fresh Strawberries: When purchasing fresh strawberries, look for plump, brightly colored berries with a strong strawberry fragrance. If prepackaged in plastic cartons, be sure to check the bottom of the container for any mushy berries or signs of mold. Store strawberries in the refrigerator and wash just before using.

Summer Fruit Punch "Salad"

PREP: 10 min. plus refrigerating • MAKES: 12 servings, ½ cup each.

WHAT YOU NEED

1 pkg. (4-serving size) JELL-O Cherry Flavor Gelatin

1 pkg. (4-serving size) JELL-O Strawberry Flavor Gelatin

1½ cups boiling water

Ice cubes

1 cup orange juice

1 pt. (2 cups) strawberries, sliced

1 cup seedless grape halves

1 cup thawed COOL WHIP Whipped Topping

MAKE IT

COMBINE dry gelatin mixes in large bowl. Stir in boiling water at least 2 min. until completely dissolved. Add enough ice cubes to orange juice to measure 2¼ cups. Add to gelatin; stir until slightly thickened. Remove any unmelted ice. Stir in fruit.

POUR into large serving bowl.

REFRIGERATE 2 hours or until firm. Top with whipped topping. Store leftover dessert in refrigerator.

Substitute: Substitute 2 pkg. (4-serving size each) **JELL-O** Mixed Fruit Flavor Gelatin for the 1 pkg. each cherry and strawberry gelatins.

Strawberry-Orange Delight

PREP: 15 min. plus refrigerating • MAKES: 16 servings, about ½ cup each.

WHAT YOU NEED

2½ cups boiling water

3 pkg. (4-serving size each) JELL-O Strawberry Flavor Gelatin

2¾ cups cold water

1 can (11 oz.) mandarin orange segments, drained

4 oz. (½ of 8-oz. pkg.) PHILADELPHIA Cream Cheese, softened

2 Tbsp. sugar

1 tub (8 oz.) COOL WHIP Whipped Topping, thawed, divided

MAKE IT

STIR boiling water into dry gelatin mixes in medium bowl at least 2 min. until completely dissolved. Stir in cold water. Refrigerate about 1¼ hours or until slightly thickened (consistency of unbeaten egg whites). Reserve a few oranges for garnish. Gently stir remaining oranges into thickened gelatin. Set aside.

BEAT cream cheese and sugar in separate medium bowl with wire whisk until well blended. Gently stir in 2 cups whipped topping. Spoon into large serving bowl; cover with the gelatin mixture.

REFRIGERATE 2 hours or until firm. Top with remaining whipped topping and reserved oranges just before serving.

How to Soften Cream Cheese: Place measured amount of cream cheese in microwaveable bowl. Microwave on HIGH 10 sec. or until slightly softened.

Triple-Berry Cheesecake Tart

PREP: 15 min. plus refrigerating • MAKES: 10 servings.

WHAT YOU NEED

1¼ cups finely crushed vanilla wafers (about 45 wafers)
¼ cup (½ stick) butter, melted
1 pkg. (8 oz.) PHILADELPHIA Cream Cheese, softened
¼ cup sugar
1 cup thawed COOL WHIP Whipped Topping
2 cups mixed berries (raspberries, sliced strawberries, blueberries)
¾ cup boiling water
1 pkg. (4-serving size) JELL-O Lemon Flavor Gelatin
1 cup ice cubes

MAKE IT

MIX wafer crumbs and butter; press firmly onto bottom and up side of 9-inch tart pan. Place in freezer while preparing filling.

BEAT cream cheese and sugar in large bowl with electric mixer on medium speed until well blended. Gently stir in whipped topping. Spoon into crust. Top with berries. Cover and refrigerate while preparing gelatin.

STIR boiling water into dry gelatin mix in medium bowl 2 min. until completely dissolved. Add ice cubes; stir until ice is completely melted. Refrigerate 15 min., or until slightly thickened (consistency of unbeaten egg whites). Spoon gelatin over fruit in pan. Refrigerate 3 hours or until set. Store leftover tart in refrigerator.

Size-Wise: This colorful berry dessert makes a great treat to share with friends and family.

Frosty Treats

Chocolate Dream Pudding Pie

PREP: 15 min. plus freezing • MAKES: 8 servings, 1 slice each.

WHAT YOU NEED

1 cup cold milk

1 pkg. (4-serving size) JELL-O Chocolate Instant Pudding

2½ cups thawed COOL WHIP Whipped Topping, divided

1 chocolate cookie pie crust (6 oz.)

2 Tbsp. hot fudge ice cream topping

MAKE IT

POUR milk into large bowl. Add dry pudding mix. Beat with wire whisk 2 min. or until well blended. Gently stir in 1½ cups whipped topping. Spoon into crust. Cover with remaining whipped topping.

FREEZE 6 hours or until firm.

REMOVE pie from freezer about 15 min. before serving. Let stand at room temperature to soften slightly. Meanwhile, heat hot fudge topping as directed on label; drizzle over pie. Store leftovers in freezer.

Size-Wise: A slice of this pie goes a long way on chocolate flavor.

Frosty Orange Dream Squares

PREP: 15 min. plus freezing • MAKES: 9 servings.

WHAT YOU NEED

- **40 vanilla wafers, finely crushed (about 1½ cups)**
- **¼ cup (½ stick) butter, melted**
- **2 pkg. (3.4 oz. each) JELL-O Vanilla Flavor Instant Pudding (see Note below)**
- **2 cups cold milk**
- **1 tub (8 oz.) COOL WHIP Whipped Topping, thawed, divided**
- **2 cups orange sherbet, softened**

MAKE IT

LINE 13×9-inch pan with foil, with ends of foil extending over sides. Mix wafer crumbs and butter. Press onto bottom of prepared pan; set aside.

BEAT dry pudding mixes and milk in medium bowl with whisk 2 min. Stir in ½ of the whipped topping. Spoon over crust. Refrigerate 10 min. Add remaining whipped topping to sherbet; whisk until well blended. Spoon over pudding layer; cover.

FREEZE 3 hours. Use foil handles to remove dessert from pan before cutting to serve.

Note from the Kraft Kitchens: For best texture, do not prepare recipe with **JELL-O** Fat Free Sugar Free Instant Pudding.

Sparkling Lemon Ice

PREP: 20 min. plus freezing • MAKES: 6 servings.

WHAT YOU NEED

- **1 cup boiling water**
- **1 pkg. (4-serving size) JELL-O Lemon Flavor Sugar Free Gelatin**
- **1 cup cold lemon lime-flavored seltzer**
- **½ tsp. grated lemon zest**
- **3 Tbsp. fresh lemon juice**

MAKE IT

STIR boiling water into dry gelatin mix in medium bowl at least 2 min. until completely dissolved. Stir in remaining ingredients. Pour into 9-inch square pan; cover.

FREEZE 3 hours or until frozen.

REMOVE from freezer; let stand at room temperature 10 min. to soften slightly. Beat with electric mixer on high speed until smooth. Spoon into 6 martini glasses or dessert dishes to serve. Store leftovers in freezer.

Use Your Blender: Use an electric blender to beat the partially frozen gelatin mixture instead of the electric mixer.

Nutrition Bonus: Cool off with this low-calorie, fat-free lemon ice.

Special Extra: Garnish with fresh lemon slices and mint sprigs.

Cookies & Cream Freeze

PREP: 30 min. plus freezing • MAKES: 12 servings, 1 piece each.

WHAT YOU NEED

4 squares BAKER'S Semi-Sweet Chocolate

14 chocolate sandwich cookies, divided

1 pkg. (8 oz.) PHILADELPHIA Cream Cheese, softened

¼ cup sugar

½ tsp. vanilla

1 tub (8 oz.) COOL WHIP Whipped Topping, thawed

MAKE IT

MELT chocolate as directed on package; set aside until ready to use. Line 8½×4½-inch loaf pan with foil, with ends of foil extending over sides of pan. Arrange 8 of the cookies evenly on bottom of pan. Crumble remaining 6 cookies; set aside.

BEAT cream cheese, sugar and vanilla in medium bowl with electric mixer until well blended. Stir in whipped topping. Remove about 1½ cups of the cream cheese mixture; place in medium bowl. Stir in melted chocolate.

SPREAD remaining cream cheese mixture over cookies in pan; sprinkle with crumbled cookies. Gently press cookies into cream cheese mixture with back of spoon; top with chocolate mixture. Cover. Freeze 3 hours or until firm. Remove from freezer about 15 min. before serving; invert onto serving plate. Peel off foil; let stand at room temperature to soften slightly before cutting to serve.

Size-Wise: Sweets can be part of a balanced diet but remember to keep tabs on portions.

Special Extra: Drizzle serving plates with additional melted **BAKER'S** Semi-Sweet Chocolate for a spectacular, yet simple, dessert presentation.

Frozen Chocolate "Soufflés"

PREP: 10 min. plus freezing • MAKES: 8 servings, 1 "soufflé" each.

WHAT YOU NEED

- **3 cups milk**
- **1 pkg. (8-serving size) or 2 pkg. (4-serving size each) JELL-O Chocolate Instant Pudding**
- **2 cups thawed COOL WHIP Whipped Topping**
- **16 chocolate sandwich cookies, finely chopped (about 2 cups)**
- **8 maraschino cherries**

MAKE IT

POUR milk into medium bowl. Add dry pudding mix. Beat with wire whisk 2 min. Gently stir in whipped topping.

SPOON 2 Tbsp. of the chopped cookies into each of 8 (8- to 9-oz.) paper drinking cups. Cover evenly with half of the pudding mixture. Press gently with the back of a spoon to eliminate air pockets. Repeat layers. Cover with foil.

FREEZE 5 hours or until firm. Remove from freezer about 15 min. before serving. Let stand at room temperature to soften slightly. Peel away paper to unmold onto dessert plates. Top each with a cherry. Store leftovers in freezer.

Variation: Prepare as directed, using **JELL-O** Vanilla Flavor Instant Pudding and chocolate chip cookies.

Frozen Lemonade Squares

PREP: 20 min. plus freezing • MAKES: 9 servings.

WHAT YOU NEED

- **9 graham crackers, finely crushed (about 1¼ cups)**
- **⅓ cup margarine or butter, melted**
- **1 qt. (4 cups) frozen vanilla yogurt, softened**
- **6 oz. (½ of 12-oz. can) frozen lemonade concentrate, thawed**
- **½ cup thawed COOL WHIP LITE Whipped Topping**

MAKE IT

MIX graham crumbs and margarine; press onto bottom of 9-inch square pan.

BEAT yogurt and concentrate with mixer until well blended; spread over crust.

FREEZE 4 hours or until firm. Serve topped with whipped topping.

Note: Empty the remaining lemonade concentrate into small pitcher. Stir in 1½ cans water. Refrigerate until ready to serve over ice in tall glasses.

Size-Wise: Looking for a special treat? Try a serving of this frosty lemon dessert.

Special Extra: Garnish with fresh mint sprigs and lemon slices.

Healthy Living

Low-Fat Strawberry Shortcut

PREP: 15 min. • MAKES: 12 servings.

WHAT YOU NEED

1½ qt. (6 cups) strawberries, sliced

¼ cup sugar

1 pkg. (13.6 oz.) prepared fat-free pound cake, cut into 12 slices

1 tub (8 oz.) COOL WHIP FREE Whipped Topping, thawed

MAKE IT

TOSS strawberries with sugar; let stand 10 min. or until sugar is dissolved, stirring occasionally.

CUT each slice of pound cake horizontally in half. Place 1 cake slice on each of 12 dessert plates.

TOP each with about ¼ cup of the strawberries and 2 Tbsp. whipped topping. Repeat layers. Serve immediately.

Nutrition Bonus: This luscious dessert is low in fat, cholesterol free and an excellent source of vitamin C from the strawberries.

NUTRITION INFORMATION PER SERVING: 170 calories, 1.5g total fat, 1g saturated fat, 0mg cholesterol, 120mg sodium, 36g carbohydrate, 2g dietary fiber, 30g sugars, 2g protein, 0%DV vitamin A, 80%DV vitamin C, 2%DV calcium, 6%DV iron.

Cool Yogurt Smoothie

PREP: 5 min. • MAKES: 4 servings, 1 cup each.

WHAT YOU NEED

- **1 container (6 oz.) strawberry low-fat yogurt**
- **1¾ cups thawed COOL WHIP FREE Whipped Topping, divided**
- **2 cups strawberries**
- **2 cups ice cubes**

MAKE IT

PLACE yogurt, 1½ cups whipped topping, the strawberries and ice in blender; blend until smooth.

POUR into 4 glasses. Top each with remaining whipped topping.

SERVE immediately.

Storage Know-How: Smoothie can be covered and stored in refrigerator up to 24 hours, or frozen up to 1 week. Reblend before serving. If smoothie was frozen, thaw 20 min. to soften slightly before blending.

Variation: Prepare as directed, using your favorite flavor yogurt, regular **COOL WHIP** Whipped Topping and/or frozen strawberries or any other cut-up seasonal fruit.

To Halve: Prepare as directed, cutting all ingredients in half. Makes 2 servings, 1 cup each.

NUTRITION INFORMATION PER SERVING: 130 calories, 2g total fat, 2g saturated fat, less than 5mg cholesterol, 50mg sodium, 25g carbohydrate, 2g dietary fiber, 15g sugars, 2g protein, 0%DV vitamin A, 70%DV vitamin C, 6%DV calcium, 2%DV iron.

Angel Lush with Pineapple

PREP: 15 min. plus refrigerating • MAKES: 10 servings.

WHAT YOU NEED

1 can (20 oz.) crushed pineapple in juice, undrained

1 pkg. (3.4 oz.) JELL-O Vanilla Flavor Instant Pudding

1 cup thawed COOL WHIP Whipped Topping

1 pkg. (10 oz.) round angel food cake, cut into 3 layers

1 cup mixed berries

MAKE IT

MIX pineapple and dry pudding mix. Gently stir in whipped topping.

STACK cake layers on plate, spreading pudding mixture between layers and on top of cake.

REFRIGERATE 1 hour. Top with berries.

Variation: Prepare using 1 pkg. (1 oz.) **JELL-O** Vanilla Flavor Fat Free Sugar Free Instant Pudding and **COOL WHIP LITE** Whipped Topping.

How to Cut Cake: Use toothpicks to mark cake into 3 layers. Use a serrated knife to cut cake, in sawing motion, into layers.

Lemon-Berry Lush with Pineapple: Prepare using **JELL-O** Lemon Flavor Instant Pudding.

NUTRITION INFORMATION PER SERVING: 160 calories, 1.5g total fat, 1g saturated fat, 0mg cholesterol, 360mg sodium, 37g carbohydrate, 1g dietary fiber, 33g sugars, 2g protein, 0%DV vitamin A, 20%DV vitamin C, 4%DV calcium, 2%DV iron.

Easy Pudding Milk Shakes

PREP: 5 min. • MAKES: 5 servings, 1¼ cups each.

WHAT YOU NEED

- **3 cups cold fat-free milk**
- **1 pkg. (4-serving size) JELL-O Chocolate Fat Free Sugar Free Instant Pudding**
- **3 scoops (about 1½ cups) fat-free no-sugar-added vanilla ice cream**

MAKE IT

POUR milk into blender. Add dry pudding mix and ice cream; blend on high speed 15 sec. or until well blended.

SERVE immediately. (Or, refrigerate until ready to serve, stirring just before serving. Mixture thickens as it stands. Thin with additional milk, if desired.)

Variation: Prepare as directed, using 2% or whole milk, regular **JELL-O** Instant Pudding and your favorite flavor of regular ice cream.

Substitute: Prepare as directed, using **JELL-O** Vanilla Flavor Fat Free Sugar Free Instant Pudding.

Nutrition Bonus: An updated version of an old-time favorite, this creamy milk shake is low fat, saturated fat free and an excellent source of calcium.

NUTRITION INFORMATION PER SERVING: 130 calories, 1g total fat, 0g saturated fat, less than 5mg cholesterol, 360mg sodium, 25g carbohydrate, 0g dietary fiber, 10g sugars, 7g protein, 8%DV vitamin A, 2%DV vitamin C, 20%DV calcium, 2%DV iron.

Special Extra: Garnish each with a dollop of thawed **COOL WHIP** Whipped Topping just before serving.

Index

Angel Lush with Pineapple........60

Banana Cream Pie
with Caramel Drizzle...............30

Banana Split Pie.........................14

Chocolate-Dipped
Strawberries...........................36

Chocolate Dream
Pudding Pie 44

Cookies & Cream Freeze...........50

Cool Raspberry Fruit Dip...........32

COOL WHIP Cookie
Sandwiches 24

Cool Yogurt Smoothie 58

Easy Pudding Milk Shakes.........62

Firecracker Bites 8

Floating Fruit Parfaits................34

Fourth of July Party Trifle............2

Frosty Orange Dream
Squares...................................46

Frozen Chocolate "Soufflés"......52

Frozen Lemonade Squares........54

Low-Fat Strawberry
Shortcut..................................56

Luscious "Cream Puffs" 16

Melon Bubbles 22

Patriotic Gelatin in a Cloud..........4

Patriotic Poke Cake 10

Rocket Pops 6

Sparkling Lemon Ice..................48

Strawberry-Mango No-Bake
Cheesecake 18

Strawberry-Orange Delight.......40

Summer Berry
Cheesecake Pie 20

Summer Fruit Punch
"Salad"....................................38

Triple-Berry Cheesecake
Tart 42

Triple-Layer Lemon
Meringue Pie 26

Tropical Pina Colada Pie............28

Wave Your Flag Cheesecake 12